Hi!

Thank you so much for purchasing my coloring book.

Coloring tips:
- Use a blank sheet of paper behind each page so the colors
  don't bleed through.
- The empty pages at the end of the book can be used to
  test & sample your colors.
- You can also color digitally - digital coloring pages
  are available at my website www.durianaddict.com.
- Cover art is colored digitally in Procreate. Two coloring pages
  were combined to create the cover design.

Please share your coloring on social media and tag @durianaddict.

Happy coloring!

-T

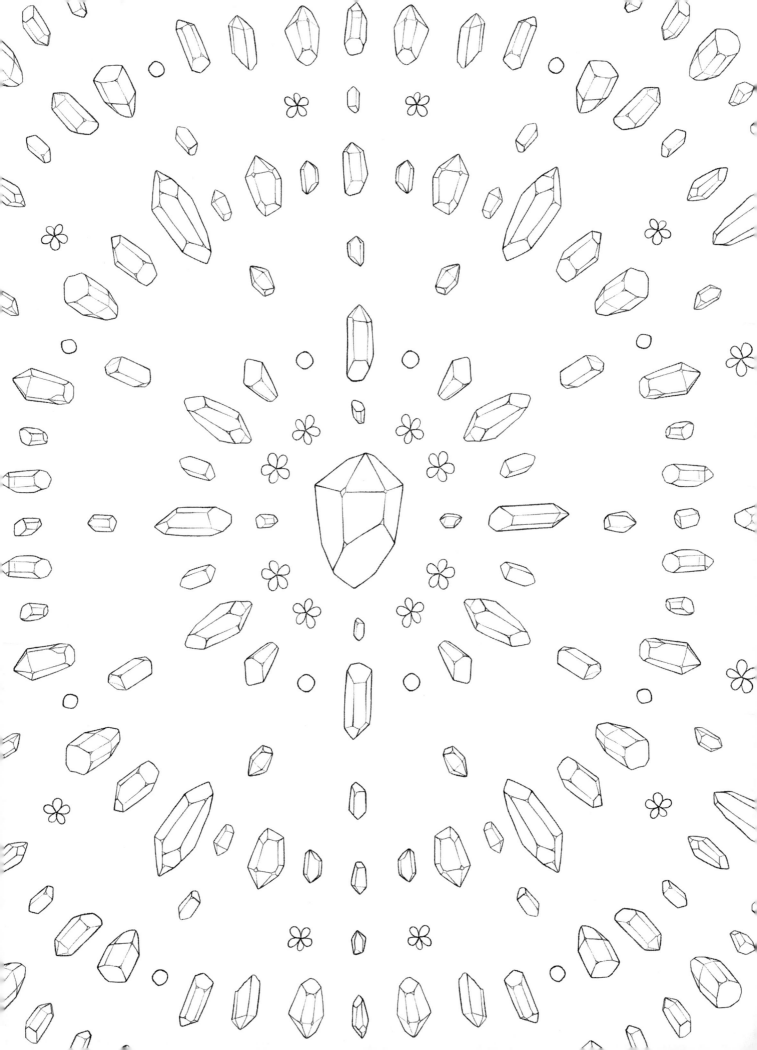

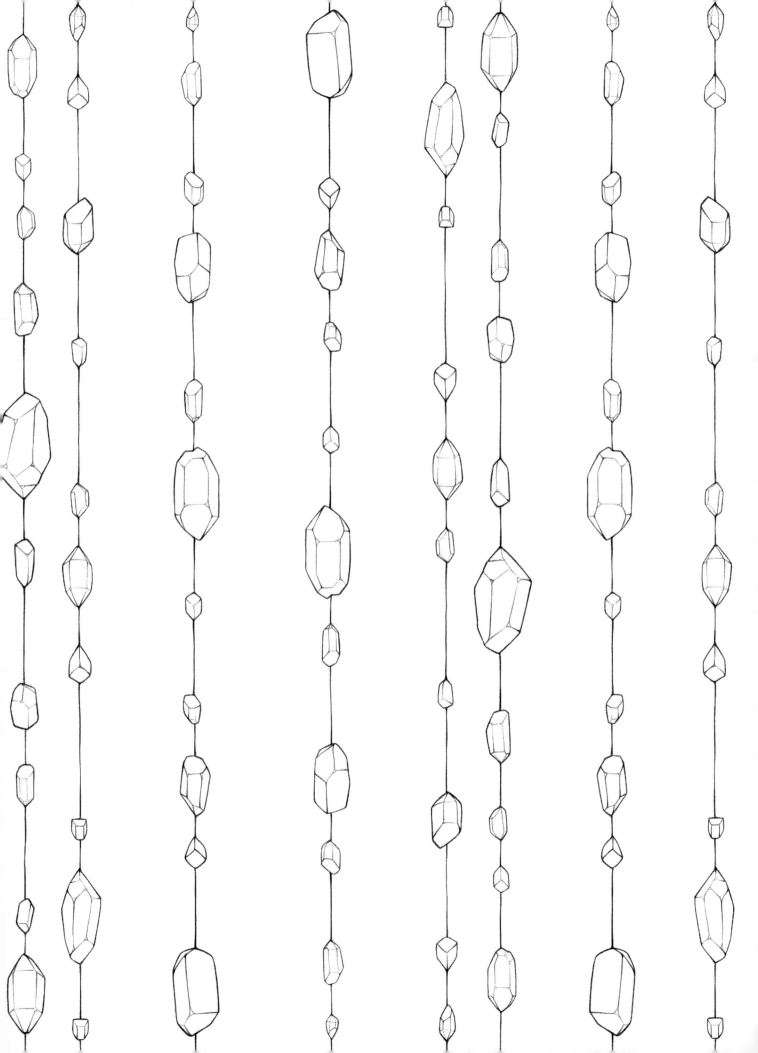

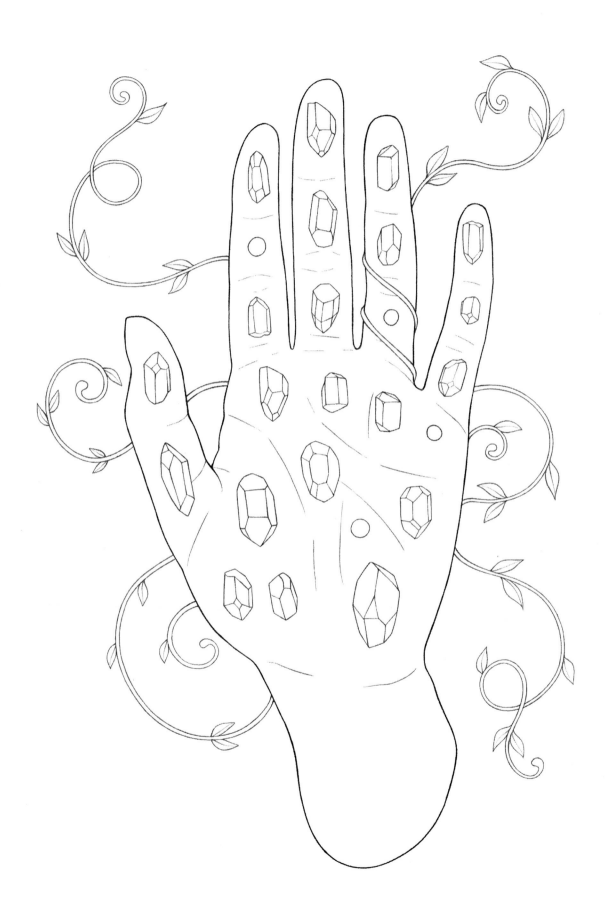

Made in United States
North Haven, CT
17 April 2022